W9-DHX-721

HOME

Vol. 46, No. 5

Publisher, Patricia A. Pingry
Executive Editor, Cynthia Wyatt
Art Director, Patrick McRae
Production Manager, Jeff Wyatt
Editorial Assistant, Kathleen Gilbert
Copy Editors, Marian Hollyday
　　　　　　　 Rhonda Colburn

ISBN 0-8249-1075-3

IDEALS—Vol. 46, No. 5 August 1989 IDEALS (ISSN 0019-137X) is published eight times a year: February, March, May, June, August, September, November, December by IDEALS PUBLISHING CORPORATION, Nelson Place at Elm Hill Pike, Nashville, Tenn. 37214. Second class postage paid at Nashville, Tennessee, and additional mailing offices. Copyright © 1989 by IDEALS PUBLISHING CORPORATION. POSTMASTER: Send address changes to Ideals, Post Office Box 148000, Nashville, Tenn. 37214-8000. All rights reserved. Title IDEALS registered U.S. Patent Office.

SINGLE ISSUE—$3.95
ONE-YEAR SUBSCRIPTION—eight consecutive issues as published—$17.95
TWO-YEAR SUBSCRIPTION—sixteen consecutive issues as published—$31.95
Outside U.S.A., add $6.00 per subscription year for postage and handling.

ACKNOWLEDGMENTS

HIGH FROM THE EARTH I HEARD A BIRD by Emily Dickinson. Reprinted by permission of the publishers and the Trustees of Amherst College from THE POEMS OF EMILY DICKINSON, Thomas H. Johnson, ed., Cambridge, Mass.: The Belknap Press of Harvard University Press, Copyright 1951, © 1955, 1979, 1983 by the President and Fellows of Harvard College; KEEPING HOUSE by Edgar A. Guest from LIVING THE YEARS, Copyright, 1949, by The Reilly & Lee Co. Reprinted by permission; NOCTURNE: GEORGIA COAST from NEVER THE NIGHTINGALE by Daniel Whitehead Hicky. Reprinted from The Saturday Evening Post © 1951 The Curtis Publishing Co. Reprinted by permission; A HOME WHERE I STAYED from AUNT HATTIE'S PLACE by Edna Jaques, Copyright, 1941 and FARM KITCHEN from THE GOLDEN ROAD by Edna Jaques, Copyright ©, 1953, by Thomas Allen, Ltd., CANADA. Reprinted by permission; THE HAPPIEST DAYS and HOME from THE HEART CONTENT, Copyright, 1926, 1927 by Douglas Malloch. Reprinted by permission; AUGUST SUNSET from AN OLD CRACKED CUP by Margaret Curry Rorke, Copyright © 1980 by Norwood Institute Press, Midland, MI; THE LITTLE WORLD OF HOME from MOMENTS OF SUNSHINE, Copyright © 1974 by Garnett Ann Schultz. Reprinted by permission. Our sincere thanks to Helen Monnette for LILIES whose address we were unable to locate.

Typesetting by The Font Shop, Nashville, Tennessee

Four-color separations by Rayson Films, Inc., Waukesha, Wisconsin

Printing by W.A. Krueger Company, Brookfield, Wisconsin

The paper used in this publication meets the minimum requirements of American National Standard for Information Sciences—Permanence of Paper for Printed Library Materials, ANSI Z39.48-1984.

Photo Opposite
MAXWELL HOUSE
GEORGETOWN, COLORADO
Bob Clemenz

Front and back covers
PEACHAM, VERMONT
Dick Dietrich

The Little World of Home

Garnett Ann Schultz

There is a little world of home
Where loving hearts shall dwell;
'Tis here we find a beauty real
We know and love so well.
It demands the best within us,
For unless we here succeed,
We will ever be a failure
In all other words or deed.

Within our little world of home,
'Tis hard to be a saint,
For here is where we grumble most
And often voice complaint;
'Tis here we live and work and play,
Where life brings each new test,
The place where hopes and dreams are born
With those we love the best.

Oh, lovely little world of home,
Though trials may oft arise,
We find the miracles of life
Before our very eyes;
'Tis here success must surely come
If we'd succeed at all,
Within the arms of those they love,
So many rise or fall.

Rich thoughts are born, a courage real,
Perhaps a heartache too;
'Tis here we plan a way of life
And cherish dreams come true;
Sweet memories from childhood days
We treasure as our own,
And know that life is dearest in
The little world of home.

The Quiet August Noon Has Come

From "*A Summer Ramble*"

William Cullen Bryant

The quiet August noon has come;
    A slumbrous silence fills the sky,
The fields are still, the woods are dumb,
    In glassy sleep the water lies.

* * * * *

Away! I will not be, today,
    The only slave of toil and care;
Away from desk and dust! away!
    I'll be as idle as the air.

Beneath the open sky abroad,
    Among the plants and breathing things,
The sinless, peaceful works of God,
    I'll share the calm the season brings.

Come, thou, in whose soft eyes I see
    The gentle meaning of thy heart,
One day amid the woods with me,
    From men and all their cares apart.

Photo Overleaf
THE GATLISS GARDENS
KALISPELL, MONTANA
H. Armstrong Roberts, Inc.

Photo Opposite
GARDEN PATH
ST. PAUL COMO CONSERVATORY
ST. PAUL, MISSOURI
Bob Firth/Firth PhotoBank

Butterfly

Virginia Blanck Moore

Like a winging flower
The butterfly drifts by,
Yellow as a daffodil,
Softer than a sigh.

8

Photo This Page
THE BLACK SWALLOWTAIL
Ina Mackey

The blossom that it lights upon
Doesn't sway at all.
It seems to hold its breath to think
Such beauty's come to call.

And then as gently as it came,
The butterfly takes flight,
And I watch this small enchanter
Until it drifts from sight.

Roadside Flowers

Bliss Carmen

We are the roadside flowers,
Straying from garden grounds;
Lovers of idle hours,
Breakers of ordered bounds.

If only the earth will feed us,
If only the wind be kind,
We blossom for those who need us,
The stragglers left behind.

And lo, the Lord of the Garden,
He makes His sun to rise,
And His rain to fall like pardon
On our dusty paradise.

On us He has laid the duty—
The task of the wandering breed—
To better the world with beauty,
Wherever the way may lead.

Who shall inquire of the season,
Or question the wind where it blows?
We blossom and ask no reason,
The Lord of the Garden knows.

Photo Opposite
PAINTED DAISY
Gene Ahrens

Lilies

Helen Monnette

Did some star in ancient glory
Condescend to be a flower?
Is the lily's lustrous lighting
But a burning shooting star?
Or did a splash of melting gold
Congeal upon a soaring stem,
Wishing it could be a star
In the evening's diadem?

12

Photo Opposite
GOLDEN SPIDER LILIES
Fred Sieb Photography

My Neighbor's Porch

Alexandra Gabriel

Joanna fills her porch with flowers,
And flowers make us welcomed guests
Even before we enter into
Joanna's loving, cheerful nest.

Joanna knows the finest greeting
Is beauty's welcome to the eye;
She shares her flowers through the season
With all her neighbors who pass by.

I thank Joanna for the mornings
When I pass her flowery display,
And for the evenings, walking home,
My heart worn by the grinding day.

Each petal is a flag of welcome,
Each bright green leaf a badge of cheer.
Her living room goes to the road
And beckons all: ''Come visit here.''

THE WELCOMING FRONT PORCH
BRIDGTON, MAINE
Dick Dietrich

Outside a Cabin Door

Agnes Davenport Bond

I stood outside a cabin door
Far up within the mountain heights;
I saw the peaks I would explore,
Then turned my eyes from woodland sights
And watched a thin blue curl of smoke
Ascending from the cabin flue.
I watched it rise with upward stroke
Until it faded from my view.

I thought of hopes and fond desires
That often fade like smoke in air,
And wondered if their dying fires
Might be rekindled yet somewhere.
How like the smoke in boundless skies
That finds its way through cosmic bars,
Undaunted purpose never dies
But seeks its goal among the stars.

Photo Opposite
AMERICAN HERITAGE
RESTORED BOYHOOD HOME OF ABRAHAM LINCOLN
HODGENVILLE, KENTUCKY
Ken Dequaine

Coming Home

Garnett Ann Schultz

The nicest part of any trip,
No matter where we go,
Is always coming home again
To folks we love and know.
Vacation trips can bring delight;
We love to pack and leave
And travel off to unknown parts
For gladness we receive.

Now life can get monotonous—
The sameness every day,
To chat and talk to those we know
And meet along the way.
We long for strange and different things,
Somewhere our hearts can dream;
But soon we look to home again,
The old familiar scene.

The homey language is the best,
The home folks more worthwhile;
No matter what the day may bring
'Tis here we find a smile,
The gentle hearts and waiting arms
So much our very own,
A comfort when our minds are tired
To know we're coming home.

Perhaps this is the reason why
We like to take a trip,
And why we get the road maps out
And pack our trunk or grip.
We want to share the biggest thrill
Our hearts have ever known,
To hurry into waiting arms
So glad we're coming home.

Little Street

LaVerne P. Larson

All across this land of ours
Are little streets like mine,
Where homes are snuggled side by side
And where the lamplight shines.

Here people work and plan and dream
Through all the passing years;
Yes, little streets and cozy homes
Know much of joy and tears.

Happy, carefree children play
And lasting friends are made;
Though feet may roam in later years
These memories will not fade—

Mother's meals, the cookie jar,
Dad's understanding ways,
The precious golden hours
Of happy, bygone days.

How good to have a little street
To call your very own,
Where hearts find lasting happiness
And seeds of love are sown.

Martha's House

Cynthia Wyatt

The house in which Martha Anderson was born, the house her grandfather built and in which her mother lived until she died, was surrounded by twenty acres of South Carolina, a gracefully rolling land where the stony hillsides are full of cedars.

It is a beautiful house. Martha's grandfather was a shipbuilder by trade when he came to America from England, and you could see the shipbuilder's touch in the slatted window shutters and handsome ceiling beams in the downstairs rooms. He built the first house in the county to have a bay window and a cushioned window seat in the front parlor, which many young readers and dreamers appreciated over the years. He remembered the little houses which dotted the rocky coast of England where fishermen's wives watched for their husbands' safe return from the sea, and built a widow's walk at the top of the house. It was another first for the county because they were over 100 miles inland. Martha remembered gazing out over the fields as a child from the tiny rooftop perch. In those days, she did not know what a widow was.

Grandfather called his house "Our family's port in the storm." And through storms and joys of life, a port it was. When Martha fell in love and married, the ceremony was held in front of the hearth of that house, and her daughter, Ruth, named after her grandmother, was born in an upstairs bedroom.

Martha and her husband, Walter, spent many happy years there. Walter was almost as good at fixing things as Martha's grandfather had been at building them. He never allowed a broken hinge or drooping gutter to go unattended.

All was well until it came to pass that Walter was offered a good job as director of sales at a large machine manufacturer in Greenville, South Carolina, and accepted it. "What will we do with our house?" she asked him that evening after dinner. She could feel her mother's spirit in the room, nervously smoothing the napkins back into place on the table and absently adjusting the silverware as Martha was doing herself. Walter assured her that things would work out. With great sadness, Martha made plans to move.

One of their neighbors offered to buy the place on condition that Martha have the chance to buy it back again anytime she wanted to return. Martha was sick at the idea of her home passing from family hands, but thanked her neighbor and said she would talk to Walter about it. That evening, she couldn't bring herself to bring up the subject of selling, so it seemed a God-send when the next day Sam, a distant cousin who had recently moved to town, offered to live in the house. In return he would keep the place in order and work with the neighboring farmers who rented the Andersons' fields for their soybean and corn crops.

All Martha really knew about Sam was that he had spent his childhood in Atlanta, where his mother worked as a secretary. Word was that he had never "found himself." Martha hoped that Sam would be good for the house and the house would be good for Sam. On the day they left for Greenville, Sam stood in the doorway waving them on. Their hearts were heavy.

Walter's job in Greenville went well for him and the years passed. Travel home was costly, but Sam was always courteous and hospitable when they returned to drink in the familiar sights of all they loved there. Walter sent money to Sam periodically for the upkeep of the house, but there was always mending for Walter to take care of when they visited. Sam said he didn't have the knack for fixing things.

The years passed. Ruth went off to college,

and their visits home became few and far between. Martha worried when she received letters of concern from two of her old neighbors saying that they didn't like the way Sam was running the place. Walter promised that they would visit soon to see for themselves.

But they never made that trip together. Walter died suddenly of heart failure while helping to move in a new shipment at work. It was a stormy time for Martha, and her soul ached for her old friends and the familiar sights of her childhood; so she wrote to Sam to tell him she was moving back home again. After three long weeks, there was no reply. One cold November morning, Martha drove out to see him.

Despite the barren trees and iced-over fields, she felt warmed from within when she rode up the long dirt road to the house which sat on the hill. She remembered cheerful evenings with her mother in the kitchen, cleaning the dishes and pans from a comfortable family dinner, and the many happy times she had shared there with Walter. She was home!

When she knocked, there was a long wait before Sam came to the door. He stood square in the doorway and did not let her pass.

"Didn't you get my letter?" she said, surprised that he did not welcome her in from the cold. He glared at her.

"You know that Walter passed away," she said nervously. "I'm coming back home. I wrote to tell you—to give you some notice . . ."

"I'm not leaving," he said, staring past her into the cold morning light. "This place is mine now."

"How?" she asked. "How can it be yours?"

"It's mine, that's all," he said. "Go ask your fancy banker friend. He'll tell you this place belongs to me." At that he closed the door—her grandfather's fine hand-hewn door—and left her on the cold porch.

Martha was shaking when she told her story to Davis at the bank. Davis had been their family banker for over twenty years.

"Martha," he said quietly, "we know what he's done, and there's nothing we can do about it. He's been paying the taxes on the land in his own name for the past five years."

"The past five years!" cried Martha. "What does that mean?"

"Legally, it belongs to him now. It's the law. None of us realized what he had done until he asked for a loan and offered the place as collateral. Well, I can tell you, he didn't get the loan."

"But Walter sent him the tax money. It was *our* money. It's *our* home." Davis assured her there was nothing anyone could do.

Martha moved back home anyway, found a place to rent in town, and she got a job working at the post office. She took comfort in the fine old friends and neighbors who opened their hearts to her. When she visited along the road where her grandfather's house stood, she looked at the tiny widow's walk with longing.

The townfolk did not take kindly to what Sam had done. There was no longer any welcome extended to him when he shopped in town. The neighboring farmers let his fields lie fallow and would do no business with him. Eventually he lost his job in town at the gas station and it was easy to see that he was letting the house run down. He got into some trouble with the local police for public brawling. Shortly after that, he left town. No one was surprised that he left a pile of unpaid bills. To settle Sam's accounts, the house was put up for absolute auction.

On a bright, windy August morning, it seemed the whole town had assembled on the hillside in front of the house. When the auctioneer took his place, Martha's friends and neighbors grew hushed.

"Twenty acres and a house. What am I bid?"

Martha alone raised her hand.

"One thousand dollars," she said in a hesitant voice. It was all she had.

The auctioneer acknowledged her bid without ceremony. "Do I hear two thousand?" he intoned, getting into the swing of what he thought would be a long contest. "Do I hear a bid?" he pressed on, "I have one thousand, do I hear two?"

The hillside was silent. As if of one mind, the entire town stood motionless. The auctioneer couldn't believe his eyes; but every man and woman in that crowd knew what home means to the human heart. The singing of meadow birds was jubilant.

The auctioneer broke the silence, finally, and droned, "Let's be done, let's be done . . . going once . . ."

Tears flowed from Martha's eyes. She hugged all the friends who cheered with her when the auctioneer cracked his gavel with the word "Sold!"

Martha Anderson lived in the house her grandfather built until the day she died, happy, in her own bed. Ruth is raising her children there today with her husband who, like Walter before him, roams the house with hammer and paintbrush on his days off, lovingly keeping their home beautiful. Their daughter, little Martha, is known to spend hours up on the widow's walk, gazing at the rolling fields around their home, just as did her grandmother when *she* grew up in the family home, Grandfather's "port in the storm."

A CERTAIN SEASON

Henry David Thoreau

At a certain season of our life, we are accustomed to consider every spot as the possible site for a house. I have thus surveyed the country on every side within a dozen miles of where I live. In imagination I have bought all the farms in succession, for all were to be bought, and I knew their price. I walked over each farmer's premises, tasted his wild apples, discoursed on husbandry with him, took his farm at his price, at any price, mortgaging it to him in my mind; even put a higher price on it—took everything but a deed of it—took his word for his deed, for I dearly love to talk—cultivated it, and him too to some extent, I trust, and withdrew when I had enjoyed it long enough, leaving him to carry on. This experience entitled me to be regarded as a sort of real-estate broker by my friends. Wherever I sat, there I might live, and the landscape radiated from me accordingly. I discovered many a site for a house not likely to be soon improved, which some might have thought too far from the village, but to my eyes the village was too far from it. Well, there I might live, I said; and there I did live, for an hour, a summer, and a winter life;

saw how I could let the years run off, buffet the winter through, and see the spring come in. The future inhabitants of this region, wherever they may place their houses, may be sure that they have been anticipated. An afternoon sufficed to lay out the land into orchard, woodlot, and pasture, and to decide what fine oaks or pines should be left to stand before the door, and when each tree could be seen to the best advantage; and then I let it lie, fallow perchance, for a man is rich in proportion to the number of things which he can afford to let alone.

Photo Opposite
THE TRANQUIL HOME
CHOCORUA, NEW HAMPSHIRE
Dick Dietrich

Our Love Affair

Ray Koonce

I'm in love! I've been in love with old houses ever since I can remember. I have my wife's encouragement and support because she shares my weakness for mellowed brass doorknobs, well-turned balustrades, high ceilings, narrow clapboard siding, crown molding, and other characteristics of fine old homes. Wherever we have gone over the years, in this country and abroad, we have innately sought out the older homes.

With our natural propensity for the mellowness of older homes, it is not surprising that we have never lived in a new one. When years ago a job change necessitated a move to our present location, we looked for an older home for our family. My employer provided temporary housing for one year and we talked to realtors often, read newspaper advertisements voraciously, and spent many hours searching our town and the surrounding countryside for the right old house. We wanted a spacious front porch and front yard, an upstairs where beds could be left unmade without callers being privy to the fact, large rooms, period charm and adaptability to today's needs, and we wanted our home to be located in an established neighborhood.

After ten months we still had not found anything. Then one afternoon while driving down a street only a few blocks from where we were staying, the "For Sale" sign in the front yard of an older two-story home with a front porch arrested my attention. Excitedly I slammed on the brakes of the car and pulled over. I saw immediately that it had once been a home of comfort and refinement upon which many years of neglect had taken their toll. Forlorn and lonely, with scaling paint and a shabby appearance, it seemed to long for a face-lift and a new coat of paint; it seemed to long for love.

I reminded myself that when one buys a home as run-down as this one, he must have an active imagination. I allowed mine to work overtime for the rest of the week, keeping my find to myself. The following Sunday afternoon while my wife and I were in the car, I apologetically said, "I know where there is an older house, but I doubt that you'd be interested in it because it is so dilapidated." Her instant reply was, "Let's go and see it!"

As the owners showed us through all ten of the spacious but dismally dark rooms, we could feel each other's excitement mounting. We communicated our delight at what we were seeing with silent, knowing glances.

After the tour we stood on the front walk and gazed at this once attractive home, wondering if its dignity and understated charm could be restored. We could both see ways to relieve the drabness and agreed: "It's irresistible if investigation proves it to be structurally sound."

The house passed inspection. Knowing that resuscitating our patient would require patience, courage, luck, and money, we took the plunge. She became ours. That was the beginning of a romance with an old house which was to become *home* to all of us, despite the initial skepticism of our young children who said, "That old barn? Who wants to live there?" We performed operation after operation with carpentry, paint, pipe work, and wiring and brought it back to health and beauty.

Our children's disdain for "that old barn" has long since turned into affection for the home in which their fondest memories of growing up still linger. When our daughter had grown up, graduated from college, and was seriously considering marriage to a young man she had been dating for some time, we said, "Tell us what you want in the way of a wedding and where you want to have it." She said, "I've told you since I was a little girl that I want to get married right here in this living room. I want to walk as a bride down these very stairs."

Having her marriage ceremony solemnized in this house gave it added meaning and somehow sealed the vows more sacredly. It is these memorable experiences through the years which have made this house a home, a very special place for us.

The laughter and shouts of two growing children and their friends no longer ring through these rooms, but rich memories still resound throughout the house; and now there are the calls and laughter of *their* visiting children, who seem to share their parents' love for the house. As we gather around the dining table with our children and grandchildren on special days, we utter a prayer of thanksgiving for our home which has become a rallying point for renewing and strengthening our family ties. Then we say, "Thank you, God, for this family and for this house which has contributed more than its share to strengthening our bonds."

Rudyard Kipling had it right when he said:

> God gave all men all earth to love,
> But since our hearts are small,
> Ordained for each, one spot should prove
> Beloved over all.

Our family has found that spot!

Verse from The Five Nations *by Rudyard Kipling, Doubleday, Page and Company, New York, New York. Copyright 1903.*

Photo Overleaf
MACKEY MANSION
VIRGINIA CITY, NEVADA
Ed Cooper

BITS &

Home

The wide world narrows to a road,
   The wide road to a trail,
The trail a path to your abode,
   Some cabin in the vale;
The cabin narrows to a door,
   The little door is passed,
Then comes the heart you've hungered for—
   And you are home, at last!

               Douglas Malloch

Happiness grows at our own firesides, and it is not to be picked up in strangers' gardens.

               Douglas Jerrold

Philosophy is properly a homesickness, a longing to be everywhere at home.

               Novalis

Domestic happiness is the end of almost all our pursuits, and the common reward of all our pains—When men find themselves forever barred from this delightful fruition, they are lost to all industry and grow careless of their worldly affairs— Thus they become bad subjects, bad relations, bad friends, and bad men.

               Henry Fielding

This fond attachment to the well-known place whence first we started into life's long race maintains its hold with such unfailing sway, we feel it e'en in age and at our latest day.

               William Cowper

Stint yourself, as you think good, in other things; but don't scruple freedom in brightening home. Gay furniture and a brilliant garden are a sight day by day and make life blither.

               Charles Buxton

Pieces

August Sunset

A blazing, molten coin descends
Into the far horizon's slot.
That's how the great machinery vends
Another day that's steaming hot.

Margaret Rorke

"A small house is big enough for love." In great mansions, form and state tend to damp the warmth of affection. I have seen over a little house in Italy the inscription, *Domus Parva, Quies Magna*—A little house, a great quiet.

Charles Haddon Spurgeon

Domestic bliss—thou only bliss of paradise that has survived the fall.

William Cowper

A hundred men may make an encampment, but it takes a woman to make a home.

Chinese Proverb

To Adam paradise was home—To the good among his descendants, home is paradise.

Augustus W. Hare

I Love a House

Faye M. Estabrooks

I love a house where flowers bloom
Or vines grow green in every room;
Where sheer white-curtained windows bring
Bright sunshine in from spring to spring.

I love a house with shining floors,
And patchwork quilts, and louvered doors,
Where plants are hung from ceiling hooks,
And shelves are filled with treasured books.

I love a house where laughter rings
From children's play, and someone sings
A joyous song—a house with walls
Adorned with children's crayoned scrawls.

I love a house with country charm
That's snug all seasons, cold and warm,
Where love and faith and joy expressed
Make it a house that's Heaven-blessed.

Photo Opposite
SUNNY HAPPINESS
H. Armstrong Roberts, Inc.

John Slobodnik

A Slice of Life

Edgar A. Guest

"Keeping house" some lightly call it.
   "Keeping home" I'd rather hear,
Since against what may befall it
   Love must guard it, year by year.
It must keep it gay with laughter,
   And with comradeship and song,
And with faith for what comes after,
   Since no joy can last for long.

"Keeping home" needs patient labor
   And a woman's lovely skill;
Needs the art of being a neighbor
   When someone nearby is ill.

"Keeping house" is done by others
   With the strength that money hires.
"Keeping home" needs dads and mothers
   Whose devotion never tires.

Lest its growing youth forsake it,
   Love must keep it warm and bright,
And a safe, sure haven make it,
   Where all things are set aright.
"Keeping house" means sweeping, dusting.
   It is listed as a trade;
But by stout hearts and by trusting,
   The enduring home is made.

Edgar A. Guest began his illustrious career in 1895 at the age of fourteen when his work appeared in the Detroit Free Press. *His column was syndicated in over 300 newspapers, and he became known as "The Poet of the People." Mr. Guest captured the hearts of vast radio audiences with his weekly program, "It Can Be Done" and, until his death in 1959, published many treasured volumes of poetry.*

Farm Kitchen

Edna Jaques

The kettle sings a low, contented tune.
    The dog snores in her sleep behind the stove;
There is a mingled odor in the air
    Of apple pie and cinnamon and clove—
The smell of yeast . . . for Mother set the bread
    In the blue pan before she went to bed.

Beyond the pantry door, I catch a glimpse
    Of shiny milk pans on a narrow shelf,
A row of plates . . . the old brown cookie crock;
    A brimming water pail all by itself;
A little bracket lamp beside the door
    Makes a small halo on the kitchen floor.

An old grey cat is sleeping on a chair,
    Paws folded in below her snowy chest.
She looks the picture of contented peace,
    Like an old lady waiting for a guest.
Her eyes blink softly as if half awake,
    Pale green, like water in a mountain lake.

The kitchen has a fragrance of its own
    Of porridge simmering in a blue pot,
Of kindling wood drying beneath the stove,
    And red coals glowing beautiful and hot.
There is a sense of joy and comfort there
    In the old stove and cushioned rocking chair—

A feel of home and peace and fireglow
That lovely modern kitchens do not know.

Photo Opposite
KITCHEN, GOVERNOR GOODWIN MANSION
STRAWBERRY BANKE
PORTSMOUTH, NEW HAMPSHIRE
Laatsch-Hupp Photo

A Home Where I Stayed

Edna Jaques

A little bureau painted white,
    Blue paper on the bedroom walls,
A sunny kitchen warm and clean,
    A room where sunlight brightly falls,
Some little knickknacks here and there,
    Wide arms upon a rocking chair . . .

Her meals are always piping hot;
    No matter what she serves it's good—
Old-fashioned stew, salt rising bread.
    The little shiny stove burns wood,
The air is fragrant as a church,
    Tamarack and spruce and silver birch.

Her man comes in all tired out,
    Slips off his shoes to ease his feet;
She fusses over him a bit,
    Has something that he likes to eat
All ready to dish up and hot
    And pours it steaming from the pot.

After the meal, he is content
    To talk about the news of town,
Turns on the radio and reads,
    Then lights his pipe to settle down,
Smoking a faint, clean-smelling stuff—
    A slow content in every puff.

The "little people," strong as steel,
Who keep the world on even keel.

As the memories of antique irons in actual use fade, collectors are beginning to look upon these homely artifacts with increasing favor. Often the old irons are notable for their charm, beauty, and naive inventiveness of design. In fact, good examples of antique pressing irons are becoming scarce, but today's prices still seem modest to the serious collector.

The majority of antique pressing irons, however, were heated on stoves or hearths before use. The most well-known type of antique iron, the common sadiron ("sad" is an archaic word meaning heavy), better known as a flatiron, was in general use during the nineteenth and early twentieth centuries. For all its simplicity, the flatiron, made of solid metal and heated on a stove or hearth, persists as the foundation of most collections. Flatirons were often cast with the maker's name and a number indicating the approximate weight. The weight of an iron was important. More delicate fabrics and intricate tuck work, such as that found on fancy shirt fronts, required lighter irons than did heavier fabrics. A collector's pride and joy is a complete set of irons in graduated sizes.

As one heated the iron, of course, one also heated the handle. This serious problem of untouchable handles spawned a plethora of imaginative iron designs. Various methods of air-cooling involved riddling the handle with holes or slots. One approach much appreciated today for its looping design and bold concept is W. M. Ferris's Cold Handle Iron, patented in 1891. The handle was made of a spiral rod, coiled like a spring, and was long enough to dissipate heat and keep hands a sufficient distance from the hot iron itself.

Nineteenth-century inventors labored to perfect the concept of a flatiron with a detachable handle. A removable handle required a simple yet reliable release since handling a hot iron could be a dangerous undertaking. Early attempts to create a detachable handle resulted in muddled efforts, but the final answer was achieved by Mary Florence Potts in her

A pyramid heater and a variety of sadirons

Although they have played an indispensable role in helping to groom our wardrobes, pressing irons have been symbols of drudgery for centuries and to this day suffer from an image problem. Memories persist of sweltering labor and aching muscles from bending over an ironing board with a stove-heated iron in hand, trying to master the delicate business of not overheating irons on the stove and of getting the most out of them before they cool off. Fortunately, today's realities are different. No-iron fabrics and friendlier, lightweight electric irons have lessened the household ironing chore.

The Manville Fluter for cranking out yards of ruffles

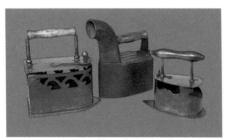
Charcoal irons: French, American, and Dutch

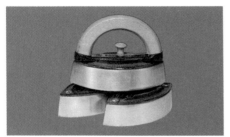
Irons in the style of Mrs. Potts's designs

famous patent of 1871. She devised a semicircular wooden handle which stayed cool. The iron was pointed on both ends so it could be used equally well in either direction, a feature common to many flatirons. Her irons were licensed to the Enterprise Manufacturing Company of Philadelphia and became known throughout the world as Mrs. Potts's Irons.

Charcoal-burning irons produced heat from live coals inserted in hollow chambers within the body of the iron. Conceived as a small flat-bottomed stove with a handle, seventeenth-century models are still to be found by collectors today. The French *fer bateau*, which literally means "iron boat," is a sheet iron charcoal-burner made prior to common use of the cast flatiron. There are still fine handmade pieces around today which may be two or three hundred years old.

During the same historical period as the *fer bateau*, Dutch artisans made charcoal irons from sheet brass with an iron sole. The classic Amsterdamer pattern was characterized by a single ventilation hole on each side and a thorn latch. In the eight-

een hundreds, the design changed to what is called the Hollander type, which had a brass sole, bell-shaped ventilation holes, and a clothespin latch.

With the advent of cast iron, industry enthusiastically strove for greater user-comfort by adding dampers, heat shields, and chimneys. The American inventive genius tacked on its usual quota of "bells and whistles." Ash catchers were introduced, and grates and rotating dampers enhanced the glitz.

Another exclusive American device was the hand fluter. Cloth for collars and cuffs was ruffled with a heated corrugated base and a rocker or gear-like roller. Hand-cranked fluters came along soon after and an example is shown in the Manville Fluter, which resembles a modern pasta machine. These mechanical fluters marked the final evolution of the European poking stick which was used centuries ago for setting the elaborate ruffs worn by royalty. Today poking sticks are prized collectibles.

The hobby of collecting antique pressing irons is becoming more popular as the variety and excitement is recognized. Choices abound for every taste; from sadirons, fluters, and charcoal irons to the earliest electric irons. Some people collect nothing but miniature irons. Whatever the category, collectors will find plenty to love.

Carol and Jimmy Walker

Carol and Jimmy Walker live in Waelder, Texas, and have written articles about iron collecting for The Antique Trader Weekly, Antiques and Collecting, *and* Women's Household.

Poking sticks used to set royal ruffs

Photography by Carol Walker

Friendly Old Houses

Elisabeth Weaver Winstead

I like old houses with shutters that sag,
And a split-rail fence that runs zigzag
Like racing children playing tag—
Friendly old houses with steps worn thin
By bustling feet that walk out and in.

I like old houses that shine in the rain,
That shoulder the storm and shelter the pain
Of watching for loved ones, sometimes in vain—
Happy old houses that toast in the sun
To brown like a crusty, freshly-baked bun.

I like old houses that peacefully wait
For the clasp of hands on the creaking gate,
Knowing friendship and love are never too late—
Rambling, rare houses with wisdom grown old,
Steeped in life's secrets forever untold.

The Happiest Days

Douglas Malloch

Sometime, someone very old,
    Walking somewhere, east or west,
With a hand to which to hold
    And a cane on which to rest,
Suddenly will stop and gaze
    All around a little while
    And will say, will say, and smile,
"Here I spent my happiest days."

Someone, sometime—maybe you,
    Thus will come upon a spot,
Come upon a place you knew
    That you never have forgot.

Though your back perhaps is bent,
    You will straighten up a bit
    And will say, beholding it,
"Here my happiest days were spent."

Sometime, somewhere—maybe now
    We are living life the best.
Care may furrow someone's brow,
    Grief may sadden someone's breast,
But you yet may backward gaze
    Down the road you walk today,
    And to someone you may say,
"Here I spent my happiest days."

Summer Shower

A sparkling summer shower
  bathed the earth today.
It wet the ground and cooled the air
  and washed the dust away.

It left the green leaves shining,
  washed flowers' faces clean,
And made the world a fresher place—
  beautiful and serene.

Eleen R. Mitchell
Columbus, Georgia

Eternal Life

With stars and suns and windswept space,
Our hearts are all aflame;
We know we live, self-conscious are,
And love God's mighty name.

We see His footprints all around,
His beauty, and His love;
We count His billion worlds
Each night we care to look above.

There is a word; there is a rule,
And God has set it so.
We have a guide for life's dark night:
The Bible's plan to follow.

Our lives are happy in His care,
We need no other god,
For He will comfort us through life
And raise us from the sod.

John W. Findley
Ava, Missouri

Reflections

SummeRetrospective

Little boys and
    Huge oak trees
Meant to climb;
    Enough of these
Filled my dreams of summer nights;
    Fading stars,
    Water fights . . .
Happy trips to summer fairs,
    Ferris wheels,
    Grizzly bears . . .
Lemonade squeezed fresh and tart
    To quench the thirst
    And please the heart . . .
Sunburned backs and
    Stinging bees,
Summertimes were
    Made of these.

Pearl Bloch Segall
Warren, Ohio

Editor's Note: Readers are invited to submit unpublished, original poetry, short anecdotes, and humorous reflections on life for possible publication in future *Ideals* issues. Please send copies only; manuscripts will not be returned. Writers receive $10 for each published submission. Send material to "Readers' Reflections," Ideals Publishing Corporation, P.O. Box 140300, Nashville, Tennessee 37214-0300.

Cupboard Cleaning

"I'll clean the cupboard this morning," I say,
"And go on a real pitchin' spree."
Then I find myself adding more things to the shelves
Because that is where they should be.
Discovering others are knickknacks from which
I just cannot bear to be parted,
I find myself finishing this hopeless task
With much more than when I first started!

E. Cole Ingle
Mansfield, Ohio

A Change of Mind

Agnes Davenport Bond

She kept her house so orderly,
So very clean and neat;
She was disturbed if one came in
With dust upon his feet.

One day her daughter's family came.
The twins were more than fair,
And she admired their winsome grace,
Their shining eyes and hair.

But they were very lively twins.
They picked the flowers in bloom.
They chased the cat and pulled her tail
And raced from room to room.

They threw the pillows off the couch;
They finger-marked the doors
And scattered cookie crumbs about
Upon the rugs and floors.

A neighbor who came in remarked,
"It cannot be denied
That children are a dreadful care;
Your patience must be tried."

"Oh, not at all," she answered then.
"What value are my rugs,
My polished floors, and costly jars
Compared to children's hugs?

"These babes are treasures of my heart,
No matter what they do."
Then quickly she made up her mind
That this was really true.

Summertime Garden Soups

Onion Soup

Serves 6 to 8

  2 tablespoons vegetable oil
  3 tablespoons butter
  4 cups thinly sliced onions
½ teaspoon salt
¼ teaspoon freshly ground pepper
¼ teaspoon thyme
  3 tablespoons flour
1½ quarts beef stock
  1 teaspoon Worcestershire sauce
  1 small loaf French bread, sliced and toasted
  8 slices Swiss cheese
    Parmesan cheese

Heat oil and butter in a large, heavy skillet; sauté onions until tender, but do not brown. Sprinkle onions with seasonings and flour; stir until flour is absorbed. Add stock and Worcestershire sauce and simmer, partially covered, until onions are cooked. Pour soup into individual crocks. Arrange toast and Swiss cheese on soup. Sprinkle generously with Parmesan cheese. Broil until cheese is melted.

Zucchini and Tomato Soup

Serves 6

  4 tablespoons butter
  2 cloves garlic, minced
  1 onion, minced
  4 medium zucchini, diced
  3 ripe tomatoes, peeled and chopped
1½ quarts beef stock
¼ teaspoon marjoram
    Cooked rice
    Grated Parmesan cheese

Melt butter in a heavy saucepan. Sauté garlic and onion over medium heat, stirring occasionally, until tender. Add zucchini and sauté until golden. Add tomatoes; simmer for 5 minutes. Blend in stock and marjoram; simmer, partially covered, until zucchini is tender (about 15 minutes). Serve with hot rice and sprinkle with grated cheese.

Cream of Spinach Soup

Serves 6

3 tablespoons butter
2 cloves garlic, minced
8 green onions, chopped
1 quart chicken stock
2 packages (10 ounces each) chopped frozen spinach,
  thawed and drained
1 large potato, grated
3 cups half-and-half
  Salt
  Nutmeg

In a large, heavy saucepan melt butter over medium heat; sauté garlic and onions until tender. Add 1 cup stock, spinach, and potato. Simmer, covered, for 15 to 20 minutes. Remove spinach mixture and puree in a blender or food processor fitted with a steel blade; return to soup. Stir in half-and-half and remaining stock and simmer for 10 minutes or until soup is warm. Season to taste.

Mushroom and Potato Soup

Serves 6

1½ quarts beef stock
  2 carrots, sliced
  1 pound mushrooms, sliced
  1 large onion, thinly sliced
  4 potatoes, peeled and sliced
    Salt and pepper to taste
  4 tablespoons butter
  3 tablespoons flour
  1 teaspoon caraway seed

Combine stock, vegetables, salt, and pepper in a saucepan. Bring to a boil over medium heat. Reduce heat and simmer, partially covered, until vegetables are tender (about 30 minutes). Melt butter in saucepan; whisk in flour until absorbed. Stir in ½ cup of the soup and cook until mixture thickens; return to soup. Simmer, stirring occasionally, until slightly thickened (about 5 minutes). Stir in caraway seed and serve hot.

50 YEARS AGO

Paris Says Corsets

But What Will the American Woman Say?

Paris has spoken. The corset is coming back. The slender waist is "in" again. Figures are the style, restrained figures with the restraint emphasized. But this is a comfortable corset, easy to wear as well as easy to look upon. So says Paris.

All of which is interesting, if true. And important to the couturiers, to the stylists, to the manufacturers and retailers, to the women—yes, and to the men.

. . . Back in the sixteenth century, the men of Austria were so beguiled by wasp waists that Emperor Joseph issued an order banning corsets in "nunneries and all places where young females are educated." He enforced the ban with the threat of excommunication, and he backed it up with a wordy warning from his Royal College of Physicians pointing out that corsets are unhealthful.

But did it have any lasting effect? It did not! The corset, in one form or another, had been in use from the days of early Rome, when the women wound themselves with broad bandages to confine unsightly bulges. In the Middle Ages they devised corsets of leather, with wooden plates up the front to give that svelte line. In France, at a somewhat later date, they made corsets with whalebone and steel for reinforcement, and during the time of Queen Elizabeth, the French dictators of fashion decreed that thirteen inches, no more, no less, was the proper circumference for the fashionable woman's waist. And women lived up to the dictum, too, confining themselves in harness and steel birdcage corsets. No woman, said an authority of the day, should risk an unfashionable "athletique" body.

But did the corsets fool the men? After a fashion, they did. A good many of the poets—and every gallant, no matter how mediocre his talent, fancied himself a poet—wrote verses about Milady's tantalizing, slender waist. But Ben Jonson wrote lines of disillusionment which ended with a salute to "the whalebone man that quilts the bodies I have leave to span." And John Gay spoke right out in meeting and left no doubt about the fact that he had been called upon once too often to give a corset string a final tug. He wrote:

I own her taper form is made to please,
Yet if you saw her unconfined by stays!

Hal Borland

50

Fashions Viewed As Plea For Peace

Lilly Daché, Back From Paris, Finds Women Using Clothes as Weapon Against War

Mme. Lilly Daché, New York millinery designer, declared yesterday on her return from Europe that the present trend in women's fashions could be attributed in some degree to woman's desire to prevent war.

"The 1939 collections prove that they are afraid of war and are using their most potent weapon, clothes, to prevent it, by appealing to men's protective instincts," Mme. Daché said.

She returned on the French liner *Normandie* after a visit to France to see the fashion openings. Miss Hattie Carnegie, couturiere, and Miss Fira Benenson, director of the salon de couture at Bonwit Teller, were others of a number of fashion leaders who came back on the *Normandie*.

Mme. Daché said that the outcome of the present difficulty in Europe would determine what clothing women finally would wear in the coming seasons. "If war breaks out," she added, "all the rich, elaborate, and regal clothes women plan will be thrown away. Instead they will wear functional, serviceable, sexless things on the order of uniforms."

Uncorseted Waist "Prettier"

Miss Carnegie said that everyone in Paris was talking about corsets and that she herself had bought some. But she added, "I can't believe American women will suddenly wrap themselves up in corsets when the uncorseted waistline is so much more natural and much prettier. . . ."

Miss Benenson said she had brought back the original Mainbocher "stem torso" corset, and that the excitement prevailing in fashion circles over the wasp waist and hourglass figures had been partly the result of exaggeration. . . ."The corset does make the waistline two inches smaller to be sure, but without discomfort or undue strain. It gives a graceful, stemlined torso which extends the waistline above and below, giving an optical illusion of extreme slimness."

UPI/Bettman Newsphotos

CRAFTWORKS

A Lovable Cat to Appliqué

This cheerful cat can be appliquéd onto ready-made garments such as the sweatshirt shown in the photograph opposite, or onto the girl's A-line jumper and boy's sunsuit made from commercial patterns. Joan Alberstadt gives instructions for lining the dress and sunsuit which gives the garments a custom-made look. Directions follow on the following page.

Materials Needed for Garment:

Commercial pattern for girl's A-line jumper or boy's sunsuit
Blue poplin—yardage indicated on pattern envelope
Blue gingham lining—same yardage as poplin
Four ½-inch buttons to match poplin
Thread to match poplin
Option: Use a purchased ready-made garment.

Materials Needed for Appliqué:

⅛ yard white poplin
⅛ yard medium- to heavyweight fusible interfacing
⅛ yard narrow pink ribbon
White thread
Embroidery floss, pink and black
White acrylic fabric paint
Small paintbrush

Photo Opposite
Gerald Koser

Step One: Cutting Fabric

Using only the front and back pieces of a commercial pattern, fold up or cut off pattern to desired hem-length of dress or sunsuit, allowing for a ⅝-inch seam. (You will not have a hem because the garment is lined.) Add 2½ to 3 inches to length of button tab on shoulder so that the garment can be lengthened as the child grows. Cut back and front from poplin and gingham.

Note: If making the sunsuit, stitch center seam of front and press seam flat before appliquéing.

Step Two: Cutting Appliqué

Using a large sheet of paper, rule off as many one-inch squares as the diagram shows. Then enlarge the pattern by drawing in the same lines as they appear in the corresponding squares of the diagram. Trace the enlarged cat onto interfacing. Following manufacturer's directions, iron interfacing to white poplin and cut out along tracing lines. Lightly pencil in facial features on the poplin cat.

Step Three: Appliquéing

Position the cat on front of garment and pin in place. Appliqué the cat's body using a wide zigzag stitch of your sewing machine. (If appliquéing by hand, baste cat in place and appliqué using two strands of embroidery floss in a close blanket stitch.)

Embroider eyes, whiskers, and mouth in outline stitch, using two strands of black floss. Or, if you prefer, you can paint the facial features with acrylic paint. Tack on a bow of narrow pink ribbon at the cat's neck for the girl's dress.

Step Four: Constructing Dress

After the appliqué is finished, sew side seams of the dress with right sides together. Press seams open. Sew side seams of lining and leave a four-inch opening in the middle of one side for turning.

Press seams open. With right sides together, pin lining to dress at neck edge. Sew around armhole, shoulder straps, and neckline. Trim and clip seams. Turn and press.

To hem, pull bottom of the garment through the side seam opening and match up lining and dress seams, right sides together. Stitch all around hem and turn right-side out through opening. Trim and press. Slip-stitch lining seam to close. Make buttonholes and sew on buttons.

Using a small paintbrush, paint paw prints (a simple oval with three small circles at one end) with acrylic paint onto the front and back of the garment.

Step Five: Constructing Sunsuit

After appliqué is finished, sew back seam and side seams right sides together. Press seams open. Sew front, back, and side seams of lining, leaving a four-inch opening in the back for turning. Press seams open.

With right sides facing, pin lining to sunsuit at neck edge. Sew around armholes, across shoulders, and around neck, leaving the crotch seam open. Then sew crotch seams, lining to lining and poplin to poplin. Turn and press. Sunsuit will now be right-side out. Working through the back seam opening, pull up both poplin and lining of one leg. Poplin and lining will be right sides together. Matching crotch seams, stitch around hemline. Clip and press. Turn right-side out through opening in lining. Repeat for second leg. Slip-stitch opening of lining to close. As with girl's dress, make buttonholes, sew on buttons, and paint paw prints with acrylic paint.

Joan Alberstadt

Joan Alberstadt owns The Cat's Meow in Nashville, Tennessee. She specializes in gifts and other treasures featuring her painting and sewing.

From *Goldilocks and the Three Bears*,
retold by Stephen Cosgrove, illustrated by Wendy Edelson.
Published by Ideals Publishing Corporation, Nashville, TN 37214

Goldilocks and the Three Bears

Once upon a time, a long, long time ago, there stood a cabin made of wood. Now in this cabin lived three bears: a big Poppa Bear, a medium-sized Momma Bear, and a teeny-tiny Baby Bear.

Late one day, the bears prepared to eat their most favorite treat, peach porridge pie. But the porridge was too hot!

They decided to take a walk down the forest path and wait for the porridge pie to cool.

A time or two later, there happened on the path a beautiful, blond-haired little girl named Goldilocks. She spied the cabin in the woods and noticed that the door had been carelessly left open.

Against everything she had learned in school, Goldilocks walked into the cabin and looked about. There she spied three chairs set before a crackling blaze in the fireplace. There was a big chair, a medium-sized chair, and a teeny-tiny chair, and all were made of wicker and wood.

She sat in the big chair, but it was too hard! She sat in the medium-sized chair, but it was too soft! Then, she sat in the teeny-tiny chair, which fit her just right. So comfortable was she that she skrinkled and scrunched about in the chair until it broke with a crickle and a crack, and she fell giggling to the floor.

It was then that she spied the peach porridge pie cooling in the bowls on the table. She tasted the porridge in the big bowl, but it was too hot! She tasted the porridge in the medium-sized bowl, but it was too cold! Then, she tasted the porridge in the teeny-tiny bowl, and it was just right. So she gobbled it up, gulpity gulp!

"Mmmm, that was good!" she said. Finally she opened a well-worn door of hickory and shiny brass, and there she spied three beds, each covered with a patchwork quilt. There was a big bed, a medium-sized bed, and a teeny-tiny bed.

Goldilocks lay on the big bed, but it was too hard! She lay on the medium-sized bed, but it was too soft! Then she lay on the teeny-tiny bed, and it was just right. She scrunched her head into the goose-down pillow and fell fast asleep.

Goldilocks had slept for ten minutes, not a minute more, when the bears rumbled back into their house after their walk in the woods.

"Hmmm!" said Poppa Bear in his big, gruff voice, "Somebody has been sitting in my chair!"

"Tsk! Tsk! Tsk!" said Momma Bear in a singsong voice. "Someone has been sitting in my chair!"

Then little Baby Bear looked with eyes opened wide and cried, "Someone has been sitting in my chair and they broke it all up!"

"Look!" growled Poppa Bear loudly. "Someone has been tasting my porridge."

Momma Bear rushed to the table. "Someone has been tasting my peach porridge too!"

It was then that poor Baby Bear cried out, "Someone has been tasting my peach porridge pie, and they ate it all up!" Unable to hold back any more, Baby Bear began to cry, and tears slipped and dripped down his fuzzy cheeks.

Poppa Bear waddled to the bedroom to get a kerchief to wipe little bear's eyes. He stopped, looked once, and then looked again. "Someone has been sleeping in my bed!" he roared.

Momma and Baby Bear rushed into the room to see what the commotion was, when Momma Bear noticed her bed too. "Fiddle dee dee!" she grumbled and rumbled. "Someone has been sleeping in my bed!"

It was then that Baby Bear, through tear-streaked eyes, spied his own bed. "Ah, ha!" said he. "Someone has been sleeping in my bed, and there she is!"

With a wink and a blink Goldilocks woke up. She leaped to the floor and skittered and scurried over and under the beds with the bears right behind. Out of the bedroom, under the table, over the chairs she ran for her life and escaped out the door never ever to return to the woods again.

There's a lesson to be learned
From this bit of folklore:
Don't enter strange houses,
And always lock your door.

CHRONICLE
————— Lansing Christman —————

Thunderstorms can be awesome and spectacular. After a long dry spell has parched our countryside, everything which grows aches for the refreshment of rain; and in August, the rain often comes with a rich ladling of wind and lightning which thrills, frightens, and inspires the thirsty earth.

There are omens in the sky that such a storm is brewing on this hot and humid August afternoon. Thunderheads build up over the western hills like an army and herald a change in the weather of the day.

Here at our place the heat intensifies. There is hardly a stir of air in this eerie quietness. The light which surrounds us has taken on the color of darkly whorled lilacs, at once bright and muted. There is no movement in grass or grain, no movement in leaf. No birds call or sing.

Coming from far away, the faint rumblings of thunder can be heard. Leaves rustle and tremble. The clouds move nearer with marshaled strength, and the roaring and rumbling become louder and more intense. Streaks of lightning begin to pierce the darkening sky with their fierce threads of white-hot fury.

As the storm reaches us, the thunderclaps become sudden, exploding blasts that literally rattle the win-

dowpanes of our home. The earth itself seems to quiver. Sheets of driving rain sweep in with clumsy, gusting winds. Trees bend and strain, their massive limbs creaking and sighing against the great force which swirls wildly around us. Steam rises from the sidewalks as raindrops pelt the sunbaked stones, and a fragrance of freshly moistened dust rises to our senses. Water gushes from the gutter spouts and races down the ditches to the lowlands, ponds, and streams with a great, turbulent splashing.

In the same rhythm with which it has arrived, the storm ebbs from our community on its ways to another. After the storm has moved on, we walk out into the hills. They are fresh and cool. The sun comes back into view in the clearing sky which is blue as indigo. The grass turns green. Withering plants and curling leaves are revived and suddenly radiant.

Birds gather on boughs and utility lines and preen themselves, secure now that the moil of wind and water has receded. They shake their wings. They carol and sing.

Maybe the birds are as grateful as we are that a summer thundershower has brought new life and freshness to tree and flower, to grain and grass and meadowland. It is as if we have witnessed creation itself, all over again, this August afternoon.

The author of two published books, Lansing Christman has been contributing to Ideals *for almost twenty years. Mr. Christman has also been published in several American, foreign, and braille anthologies. He and his wife, Lucile, live in rural South Carolina where they enjoy the pleasures of the land around them.*

Nocturne: Georgia Coast

Daniel Whitehead Hicky

The shrimping boats are late today;
The dusk has caught them cold.
Swift darkness gathers up the sun,
And all the beckoning gold
That guides them safely into port
Is lost beneath the tide.
Now the lean moon swings overhead,
And Venus, salty-eyed.

They will be late an hour or more,
The fishermen, blaming dark's
Swift mischief or the stubborn sea,
But as their lanterns' sparks
Ride shoreward at the foam's white rim
Until they reach the pier,
I cannot say if their catch is shrimp
Or fireflies burning clear.

SHRIMP FLEET AT SUNSET
DELCAMBRE, LOUISIANA
Tom Algire Photography

THROUGH MY WINDOW

Pamela Kennedy

Homeward Bound

I waved to my husband and three children as they drove away from the airport departure gate. The rear window of the car framed three little faces throwing kisses with abandon and mouthing "Good-bye!" and "I love you!"

It felt strange, leaving them even for just a week, but it was a trip I longed to make—a trip back to places and people that were a part of my past. In the scramble of everyday living, of raising kids and keeping house, of cross-country moves and constant changes, I'd lost my sense of "rootedness." I needed to go home again.

And so, with purpose and plan, I lifted my suitcase onto the scales, handed my ticket to the agent, and boarded my homeward-bound jet.

The warm Honolulu trade winds were quickly replaced by cool, sanitized "airplane air," wheezing out of little round spigots above each seat. Tourists laden with baskets and boxes and weighed down with pungent pineapples and plumeria leis jostled each other down the narrow aisles. The overhead compartments were soon stuffed with parcels and jammed shut as passengers found their seats.

About halfway back in the cabin, I located my own place, slid into the appropriate row, and sank into the seat nearest the window. As I fussed with the tray table and adjusted the seat back, there was a commotion in the aisle and a young boy was nudged into the seat next to mine. His obviously frazzled mother plopped down next to him and admonished, "Now, Brian, don't bother the lady. Just look at your books and color or something."

Brian looked at me with wide brown eyes and I winked. His tense little face relaxed a bit, and he seemed content to unload the books and toys he had brought along for the trip. I settled back with a magazine and read through the uneventful takeoff and the first hour of the flight.

Little Brian was apparently a seasoned traveler and busily occupied himself with drawings, plastic block structures, and storybooks. By the time our in-flight meal arrived, however, he was ready for some conversation.

"You going on a vacation?" he inquired.

"No," I responded, charmed by his freckled grin. "I'm just going for a short visit."

"Oh. Where are you going for your visit?" he asked.

"To a town called Kent. It's near Seattle," I replied.

"You live there?"

"No. I live in Hawaii; but Kent is my home," I explained.

Brian looked confused. "Do you have any kids or a husband or anything?"

I smiled. "Yes I do. I have three kids and a husband and everything."

"Well, where do they live?" he pursued.

"They live in Hawaii with me. We all live together in a house with swings in the backyard and big trees to climb and a beach nearby." I thought the added detail would clear up whatever confusion reigned in the little boy's obviously busy mind.

Brian pondered that new information for a moment then looked at me shaking his head. "How can you have a home in one place if your house and your kids and your swingset are someplace else?"

At this point, Brian's mother apparently decided he needed a change of scene and whisked him off to the lavatory; then she settled him in an empty window seat on the other side of the plane.

But this question played over and over in my mind like a half-forgotten melody. How was it I still considered my home to be a small town in Washington when I hadn't lived there for over twenty years? How could the home of my childhood still pull me so strongly from my home of today? I watched the pale blue rectangle of sky and clouds pass slowly by my window as I pondered Brian's words. Home, I concluded, is more than just the place where I live with my kids and my husband and my swingset. In a more fundamental sense, home is all the things that made me who I am.

Home is clear summer skies with lofty Mt. Rainier sparkling in the distance, her tumbling mantle of snow and ice a pattern of blue and white. It's walking in the woods and smelling the sweet pungency of crushed blackberries hot in the August sun. Home is a crackling fire and spicy cider in the fall and winter's icicles dripping in crystal elegance from the eaves and branches. It's spying the first robin in my favorite cherry tree and taking the first swim of the summer in a lake cold enough to take your breath away.

Home is more than house and family. It's a unique tapestry of scents and textures, places and experiences woven together to create the context of my life. Here I can walk the paths I skipped as a child and re-create the dreams I had. I can close my eyes, smell woodsmoke and be transported three decades back to the autumn of my first crush. I can touch my personal history for fleeting, delicate moments and feel the balance once again of past and present, understanding with new clarity how I reached my destination of today.

I longed to explain it all to Brian—how home can be a place where you no longer live. But I knew he wouldn't understand; not yet; for children have a future, not a past. I settled back, instead, and closed my eyes. It was good to be homeward bound once more, to seek out long-forgotten memories and become reacquainted with myself.

Pamela Kennedy is a freelance writer of short stories, articles, essays, and children's books. Married to a naval officer and mother of three children, she has made her home on both U.S. coasts and currently resides in Hawaii. She draws her material from her own experiences and memories, adding bits of imagination to create a story or mood.

High from the Earth I Heard a Bird

Emily Dickinson

High from the earth I heard a bird,
He trod upon the trees
As he esteemed them trifles,
And then he spied a breeze
And situated softly
Upon a pile of wind
Which in a perturbation
Nature had left behind.
A joyous going fellow
I gathered from his talk
Which both of benediction
And badinage partook.
Without apparent burden
I subsequently learned
He was the faithful father
Of a dependent brood.
And this untoward transport
His remedy for care.
A contrast to our respites.
How different we are!

Photo Opposite
THE EAGLE'S NEST
Gay Bumgarner

The Myth of Amherst

When Emily Dickinson died in 1886, her sister found nearly eighteen hundred poems hidden away in boxes and bureau drawers. It took the world decades to discover that the home-bound recluse was indeed a major poet, perhaps the greatest female poet to have written in English. As uniquely American in her own poetic style as was her more effusive contemporary Walt Whitman, Emily Dickinson lived the quiet life of a spinster. During her lifetime, only a few of her poems appeared in print. At one time, she told a friend she did not deem it "feminine" to publish, but this was probably Emily rationalizing the attitude of the world around her.

Emily Dickinson was born in Amherst, Massachusetts, December 10, 1830, into an exceptional family. Her father, Edward Dickinson, was one of the town's most influential men. Among his many accomplishments, he was elected to the U.S. House of Representatives and admitted to practice before the Supreme Court.

The Dickinson household atmosphere was refined and high-minded, a distillation and condensation of New England thought in a time of great optimism and innovation in American letters—the time of Emerson, Hawthorne, Thoreau, and Melville. Emily's mother was self-effacing, the complete opposite of her father. Emily once said her mother was more solicitous about the dust on the piano than about the music it could make. Of her father, Emily wrote: "He buys me many Books—but begs me not to read them—because he fears they joggle the Mind." It is clear that Emily read the books.

Given the worldliness and erudition of her father and his circle, it is a mystery that she withdrew from society completely while in her mid-twenties and retired into the security of the family mansion. She was rarely seen by outsiders over the next thirty years, even in the house. She became eccentric, writing countless letters but insisting that others address them for her. She was invariably dressed in white gowns, but required her sister to substitute for her at the fittings. At social gatherings in her home, she would make dramatic appearances, an apparition in white, and just as suddenly disappear. She loved music, but when it was played, she remained out of sight in the hall. One visitor who sang for her was sent a glass of rich sherry and a poem which had been written during the performance. Sometimes she would let down a treat on a string from her window for little children, of whom she was very fond. It was the neighborhood lore that she had not been outside her own house in fifteen years except to see a new church; and she accomplished that by slipping out at night and viewing it by moonlight.

We simply don't know why she chose to withdraw from the world. The strongest clues may be taken from the three letters addressed "Dear Master" which she wrote in her early thirties. They seem to refer to a tragic love affair which had already ended, but it is not even known whether the final drafts of the letters were ever sent. Scholars still grapple with the problem. Was it the love of a married man—the Reverend Charles Wadsworth or Samuel Bowles? Or had she invented it all with her restless and unrelenting imagination? Unlike

Miss Havisham, the famous recluse and eccentric of Charles Dickens' *Great Expectations*, who lived in a shut up house with the bug-riddled ruins of a wedding cake as a monument to her unhappy love affair, Emily Dickinson left no overt explanation. Her letters and poems raise more questions about the actual facts of her life than they answer. She died in the house where she was born, of kidney disease, May 15, 1886. She was survived by her sister Lavinia, who had done so much to make her life comfortable, and who was later to be a champion of her poems. To her community, Emily Dickinson was as much a village oddity as the fictional Miss Havisham, but Emily was not a fictional character, and the revelation of the poems shows a rich and wonderful imagination.

When Emily was thirty-one, she wrote Thomas Wentworth Higgenson, a critic she felt might have sympathy for her work, and asked him if her verse "breathed." To her disappointment, he seemed unable to encourage her to publish. Her work was too far ahead of its time, too innovative, for him to classify. Emily became reconciled to a life without publication, recognition, or fame.

Her poems are condensed, rhymed, and usually in simple four-line stanzas. But these simple hymn forms contain some of the most original poems written in the English language. Perhaps her own definition of poetry best describes the effect her work has had upon countless readers: "If I read a book and it makes my whole body so cold no fire can ever warm me, I know it is poetry. If I feel physically as if the top of my head were taken off, I know this is poetry. These are the only ways I know it."

Emily Dickinson may have secluded herself in her home, but her poems have traveled far and wide and have brought joy and wonder to the entire world. We don't know exactly when she wrote these lines, but from her quiet home in Amherst, Massachusetts, probably 100 years ago, Emily Dickinson said to us:

> The words the happy say
> Are paltry melody
> But those the silent feel
> Are beautiful—

Charles Wyatt

Michael McKeever

Riding the Rails at Disneyland

The C.K. Holiday at the Main Street Station

Whenever I am in Los Angeles with my family, we make a pilgrimage out to Travel Town in Griffith Park. Several locomotives are on exhibit along with freight cars, passenger coaches, and so on. They can be approached and touched, and assuming one is very careful, even climbed on; but they're silent and cold; their great drive wheels are silenced forever. Visiting these old locomotives is like wandering the graveyard of the elephants, looking down at their bleached bones and marveling at what great, fierce beasts they must have been.

The old trains still live, however, at Disneyland—which bring me to Ken Kohler.

Ken Kohler is a man who appreciates beauty. He appreciates the gleam of polished brass, the hiss of steam, the deep, powerful smell of hot iron. He understands that trains are at their best when they pull into the station amid clouds of steam, that conductors are supposed to carry pocket watches, and that engineers wear red bandanas. He knows that a train whistle ought to sound like a whistle and not an air horn honking at you like a goose with bronchitis.

Kohler is in charge of the Disneyland Railroad in Anaheim, California. It is a very real, working railroad complete with roundhouse, engines, rolling stock, and timetable. He is a pleasant, friendly man who is easy to talk to; but ride the Disneyland Railroad and it quickly becomes apparent that he is a man who sets very high standards.

The brasswork on each of the line's four

nineteenth-century-style locomotives is polished by hand to a high gloss. The paint, from the candy-apple red cabs to the gold stars on the drive wheel hubs, glistens in the sunlight. And the trains pull in and out of the stations as smoothly as honey dripping from a spoon.

Engineers far younger than their locomotives are trained under Kohler's tutelage. They become familiar with the intricacies of their engines and learn to respect the fine craftsmanship that went into each locomotive's construction. Only after a suitable training period as firemen do they become full-fledged engineers.

The Earnest S. Marsh

Kohler and his roundhouse crew leave nothing to chance. Throughout the night, highly-skilled maintenance crews inspect, clean, and lubricate each locomotive and car. Repairs are made, paint touched up, brasswork polished. Careful records are kept on each piece of equipment. With early morning, the process of steaming up the boilers begins. By the time Disneyland opens, the first train is already pulling into the Main Street Station.

Each of the four Disneyland locomotives is named for an executive of the Santa Fe Railroad. The first two locomotives, the E. P. Ripley and the C. K. Holiday,

All four locomotives at Disneyland roundhouse

The Fred C. Gurley at the Main Street Station

were built from the rails up for Disneyland in the early 1950s.

Walt Disney was a train buff, and both of these locomotives were enlarged versions of the crown jewel of Disney's miniature railroad which he once operated in his own backyard, a miniature $1/8$ scale steam locomotive which he named Lilly Belle after his wife, Lillian Disney. For many years the model Lilly Belle was proudly displayed at Disneyland, but has since been moved to Florida's Walt Disney World where it is on exhibit.

Not all of the Disneyland locomotives were built from scratch. In 1958 a third engine, an 1894 Baldwin, came on the Disneyland line. The battered old veteran which had served long and faithfully in the Louisiana sugarcane fields was brought to the Disney studio

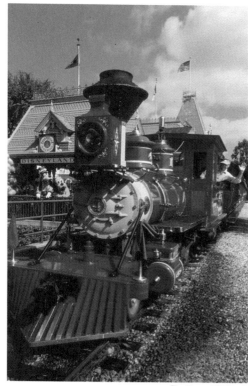

The Earnest S. Marsh

machine shop, rebuilt for a new life, and renamed the Fred C. Gurley.

A year later the Ernest S. March completed the quartet. Another old Baldwin, it had chugged through the New England woods for decades, hauling freshly cut lumber from a mill. Today it hauls passenger cars and looks as shiny as when it first rolled out of the Baldwin shops in 1925.

Accommodating millions of customers has brought inevitable changes to the Disneyland Railroad. For railroad purists, some of the changes have been painful.

At one time, each Disneyland train passenger was issued a ticket with a steel engraving of a nineteenth-century locomotive, smoke rolling majestically from its stack. At boarding time, the conductor punched

opening line from Walt Disney's 1955 welcoming speech: "To all who come to this happy place, welcome . . ." The ghostly telegrapher is still hard at work, but the little station with all its gingerbread has been moved across the tracks. In its place is a plain, though undoubtedly efficient, loading platform.

Also shunted into semi-retirement are the canary-yellow passenger coaches with their polished woodwork and intricate ceiling stencils. There were problems with their small windows and passengers preferred the open Narragansett excursion cars. Only one of the old varnish cars remains on active duty, a

The caboose, Lilly Belle

Inside the caboose, Lilly Belle

holes in the ticket, which then became a treasured souvenir. The tickets disappeared long ago into Disneyland Valhalla along with Tomorrowland's flying saucers and the Fantasyland pirate ship.

Also back in the early days of Disneyland, passengers boarding at Frontierland waited at a splendid replica of the little stations which were the pride and joy of many a prairie town. Through an open window, a phantom telegrapher endlessly tapped out the

beautifully furnished caboose named, as was Disney's original miniature locomotive, Lilly Belle. Beautifully appointed like a Victorian drawing room, the Lilly Belle caboose is an echo of a vanished era when grace and elegance rode the "High Iron." I suspect that as long as Ken Kohler is out in his roundhouse office, Lilly Belle will remain a symbol of the Disneyland line.

Over the decades, the rich and powerful and

The original Lilly Belle in Walt Disney's backyard

famous have ridden the Disneyland Railroad. Royalty, presidents, and movie stars have boarded her coaches and posed smiling in the cabs of her locomotives.

But one of the first and most special passengers was a small boy who was not famous at all.

In the early 1950s, like children all across America, he waited avidly for Disneyland's grand opening. But he was terribly ill and grew more frail with each passing day. His mother sat down and wrote a letter to Walt Disney.

Not long afterward, a locomotive eased out of the brand-new roundhouse. Aboard the train were Disney and the boy.

For a while the engine rolled along track only recently laid on the raw earth. At one point the locomotive stopped, and Disney could be seen holding the boy and gesturing at the construction still under way all around them.

Both the small boy and Walt Disney are gone now and no one knows what they talked about. But Disneyland workers remember them leaning out of

the cab as the engine moved up the track. They were laughing.

Michael McKeever is a Contributing Editor of Country Inns *magazine and a frequent contributor to* Physicians Travel. *At journey's end, Michael enjoys returning home to Imperial Beach, California.*

The Earnest S. Marsh

Photography courtesy of Disney®

Trails of Arcady

Agnes Davenport Bond

How restful are the trails which lead away
To lofty mountain peaks of blue,
Through wooded glens where ferns
Are dense beneath
The feet!

How sweet
The fragrant sheath
Along the stream that turns
And winds about to hasten through
The crooked canyons where its waters stray!
In virgin forests I would ever stay
And seek the peace of mountain view.
My craving heart discerns,
Here in this heath,
Retreat.

How fleet
By flowered wreath
Are hours in which one learns
To find the bliss he would pursue!
How restful are the trails that lead away!

Photo Opposite
BEAVER FLOWAGE AT SUNSET
GRAND TETON NATIONAL PARK
WYOMING
Tom Algire Photography

FROM MY G·A·R·D·E·N JOURNAL

Deana Deck

The Cutting Garden

Late summer is the perfect time to plan a cutting garden for next year. A cutting garden overflowing with annuals and perennials throughout the season is a double delight. It provides a bright splash of color in a corner of the yard and lets you fill your house with flowers from the earliest days of spring until the winter winds begin to howl.

To ensure a continuous supply of blooms from spring to fall, you will need a good mix of annuals and perennials. All perennials have short blooming periods, whereas annuals last for the entire season. When the perennials are finished, it's nice to have a fresh-looking, colorful annual nearby ready to be cut. Now that the fall line of perennials and bulbs are appearing at local nurseries, this is a good time to be making plans for next year's vases and flower bowls.

It is best to set out your plants in rows of graduated height. The first row will have the smallest plants and the earliest bloomers—the spring bulbs, such as daffodils, tulips, and Dutch iris. Leave space in front of the bulbs for some of the short annuals that can be picked all summer but can't be set out until late spring, like miniature snapdragons and periwinkles. Periwinkles are perky, and their thick dark leaves provide a nice background in arrangements. I like white cascading petunias too. They have longer stems than other petunias and are fragrant, delightful additions to bowls and other low arrangements.

Place mid-sized varieties in the center of the garden. Purple coneflowers, black-eyed Susans, lilies, asters, and phlox are good perennial choices. With them, mix in the best of all annuals—the zinnia. Zinnias are available in an astonishing array of colors and will bloom nonstop until winter demands that they cease.

The middle area is also a good location for irises, lilies, and gladiolus. Their tall flat leaves last most of the season and provide a calming stand of neatness against the unruly foliage of other perennials.

For fall blooms, include some asters and chrysanthemums. These can be planted in the middle of the bulb bed because they grow slowly in spring and will stay small until the bulb's blooms are long gone.

At the back of the cutting garden I put the tallest plants, such as the hollyhock, a self-seeding biennial that performs like a perennial once established. When cut, stalk and all, like a gladiolus, these are very dramatic, featured alone in a tall jar or bottle. In the garden they add an old-fashioned touch that I wouldn't be without. They remind me of cottage garden illustrations in old magazines of the 20s and 30s.

Heliopsis is another tall perennial. It adds a gorgeous splash of yellow and is long-lasting in arrangements. After blooming, it provides a dark green background for the colorful cosmos, a lovely, tall annual with feathery light green foliage.

It's helpful to include pathways in a cutting garden. The best time to pick your flowers is in the early morning when the plants are cool and fresh, and paths let you work your way through a dewy bed without getting soaked.

The easiest way to create paths is to lay strips of porous mulching fabric between rows and cover it with shredded bark. The fabric lets moisture into the soil while preventing weed growth. To water, you can just lay soaker hoses along the paths and let them drip for several hours. At the end of summer, the bark can be used to mulch the perennials against winter cold and can later be worked back into the soil as compost.

You can have blooming plants to bring indoors from Easter until the first hard frost if you plan care-

fully, and if you deadhead. It's good to know about deadheading if you think that by picking flowers and taking them inside you are doing damage. You are actually doing the plant a favor, making it more vigorous and giving it a longer lease on life. A plant's purpose in life is to reproduce itself by setting seed. Once that is accomplished, it quits producing blooms. If you pick every faded flower before the seed head forms, the plant continues to bloom for an extended period of time. It's wonderful to have a houseful of fresh flowers and feel noble at the same time!

One of the nicer aspects of having a cutting garden is that it can be tucked into a spare part of the landscape. Its ultimate purpose is to provide flowers for arrangements, and it can be installed along the alleyway or behind the garage if a flamboyant patch of color doesn't fit in with your formal landscaping.

An advantage to tucking the cutting garden out of sight is ease of maintenance. When the bulbs and perennials go into visible decline, the happy gardener can just look the other way while Mother Nature works her wonders.

My own cutting garden is right out in front. I have always loved the colorful, untamed look of English cottage gardens, and when I was looking for a sunny location, I had half the front lawn plowed up. It was an easy decision to make. I would much rather pick flowers than mow grass!

Deana Deck is a frequent contributor to Nashville *magazine, and her garden column is a regular feature in the* Tennessean. *Ms. Deck grows her cutting garden in Nashville, Tennessee.*

Photo Overleaf
MEMORIAL LIGHTHOUSE
TRINIDAD, CALIFORNIA
Tom Algire/H. Armstrong Roberts, Inc.

DAY'S END

Minnie Klemme

The ladybug's children are snug in their beds,
The bees are all back in the hive,
The cows came home by the old country lane
Sometime a little past five.

The daisies have blown and the moonflower glows,
The bluebells call curfew today,

The twilight has deepened, the first stars are out,
The children are home from their play.

Far down in the valley, a train whistles by,
A truck rumbles off down the road,
Evening has come and the traveler returns
With haste to his waiting abode.

I shall write of the day and what it has meant,
I'll pray before ever I rest,
I'll thank the Dear Lord for a beautiful day,
For day's end which always is best.

Readers' Forum

I am a true fan of Ideals *and the proud owner of the complete set, with the exception of the #5 issue—Autumn, 1945, and #20—Mother's Day, 1948. I even have the Volume I Christmas issue.*

Because life in today's world is often hectic and hurried, it always helps me to relax and enjoy a few quiet moments when the new Ideals *arrives! Keep up the good work!*

Becky Edwards
Cochranville, PA

P.S. If anyone in this great U.S.A. has either copy of Ideals *to complete my set and would be willing to sell, please let me know.*

Special opportunity to order back issues of *Ideals* **now!** From time to time we are able to offer selected back issues of *Ideals*. As a result of small overruns at the time of the original printing, a few copies still remain of earlier issues (and of course we will never be able to reprint these one-of-a-kind issues). So take this opportunity to fill in the missing issues of your *Ideals* collection or choose specific issues for friends and relatives.

ISSUES AVAILABLE

1985: Christmas—with color paintings by Robert A. Heuel . . . **Old-Fashioned**—brings back artwork by James Sessions and old-fashioned dolls . . . **Country Roads**—those old plank roads, Burma Shave signs, a beautiful tribute in photography to late summer and early fall, and *Ideals* Best-Loved Poet Mildred L. Jarrell . . . **Thanksgiving**—the pilgrims' story as told by Pamela Kennedy, *Ideals* Best-Loved Poet Mamie Ozburn Odum, and the splendor of the changing season

1986: Christmas—featuring "Annie and Willie's Prayer" by Sophia P. Snow, an *Ideals* classic . . . **Easter**—the magic of spring flowers and the story of Easter from scripture . . . **Sweetheart**—a valentine for your beloved, the story of "Love Tokens" by Frank Staff . . . **Thanksgiving**—

a charming rendition of "The Original Thanksgiving Meal"

1987: Christmas—with classic artwork by George Hinke, Frances Hook, and Sandro Botticelli . . . **Countryside**—June vacations, July 4th celebration of the blessings of liberty . . . **Mother's Day**—"Mother's Hands," "Mother's Home," and Pamela Kennedy's "Letter to My Mother-in-Law" . . . **Nostalgia**—beautiful photographs of old cars and schoolrooms, Winslow Homer's *Snap the Whip*, and "Old Things Are More Beautiful" by Clay Harrison . . . **Thanksgiving**—with "Thanksgiving Time" by Laura Ingalls Wilder and "The Lost Colony" . . . **Valentine**—heart sachets to make at home and antique Valentine's Day cards in "Collector's Corner"

To order, send the names of the issues you want with a check or money order for $3.00 for the first copy you order and $2.50 for each additional copy (postage and handling is included) to: Back Issues, Ideals Publishing Corporation, P.O. Box 148000, Nashville, TN 37214-8000. Please be sure to specify the title and year of the issues you are ordering and include your full address and telephone number with the area code.

Due to certain restrictions, we cannot service orders from outside the U.S. And remember, supplies are very limited, and unfortunately, once sold out, no issues can be reprinted. So make your requests right away.

Want to share your crafts and recipes? Readers are invited to submit original craft ideas and original recipes for possible development and publication in future *Ideals* issues. Please send recipes or query letters for craft ideas (with photograph, if possible) to Editorial Features Department, Ideals Publishing Corporation, P.O. Box 140300, Nashville, Tennessee 37214-0300. Please do not send craft samples; they cannot be returned.

ideals

Celebrating Life's Most Treasured Moments

Photo Opposite
CHICORY AND OATS
WASHINGTON ISLAND, WISCONSIN
Gene Ahrens